THE PRACTICAL STRATEGIES SERIES
IN GIFTED EDUCATION

series editors
FRANCES A. KARNES & KRISTEN R. STEPHENS

Questioning Strategies
for Teaching the Gifted

Elizabeth Shaunessy

PRUFROCK PRESS, INC.

Prufrock Press, Inc.
P.O. Box 8813
Waco, Texas 76714-8813
(800) 998-2208
Fax (800) 240-0333
http://www.prufrock.com

Contents

The Practical Strategies Series in Gifted Education offers teachers, counselors, administrators, parents, and other interested parties with up-to-date instructional techniques and information on a variety of issues pertinent to the field of gifted education. Each guide addresses a focused topic and is written by scholars with authority on the issue. Several guides have been published. Among the titles are:

- *Acceleration Strategies for Teaching Gifted Learners*
- *Curriculum Compacting: An Easy Start to Differentiating for High-Potential Students*
- *Enrichment Opportunities for Gifted Learners*
- *Independent Study for Gifted Learners*
- *Motivating Gifted Students*
- *Questioning Strategies for Teaching the Gifted*
- *Social & Emotional Teaching Strategies*
- *Using Media & Technology With Gifted Learners*

For a current listing of available guides within the series, please contact Prufrock Press at (800) 998-2208 or visit http://www.prufrock.com.

It is better to ask some of the questions
than to know all the answers.
—James Thurber

The contributions of Socrates, one of the world's most eminent philosophers, have for centuries influenced the methods for teaching higher levels of thinking. The renowned Greek philosopher engendered a spirit of inquiry through thoughtful discussions with his students, among them Plato, and perpetuated a line of thinking and teaching situated in a mindset that supports collegial, in-depth, open-minded discussion with the goal of examining the logic and reasoning underpinning all assumptions within an argument. Thus, the Socratic method was born in the second century and has withstood the test of time, informing both K–12 educators and college-level instructors. Many other avenues toward critical thinking have been forged, similar in several ways to this age-old approach, often building on the precepts of Socratic questioning.

In order to stimulate creative development among gifted students, the use of questioning techniques has proven to be a successful strategy for encouraging purposeful inquiry (Daniels, 1997; Feldhusen, 1994; Gallagher, 1985; Letzter, 1982; Parker, 1989; Pollack, 1988; Schwartz & Millar, 1996). The use of a variety of questioning strategies is recommended, focusing primarily on the higher end of Bloom's taxonomy to engage students in advanced-level thinking. Teachers can incorporate questions effectively by knowing the various purposes, types, and intended outcomes and by establishing a classroom climate that promotes active engagement, exploration, and inquiry to further student achievement.

Why Ask Questions?

To the dismay of many educators and potential employers, it is daunting how few students are able to "draw inferences from texts, distinguish the relevant information in mathematics problems, or provide and defend a thesis in an essay" (Wolf, 1997, p. 10). While researchers indicate that questioning strategies are essential to the growth of critical thinking skills, creative thinking skills, and higher level thinking skills (Daniels, 1997; Gallagher, 1985; Letzter, 1982; Parker, 1989; Pollack, 1988; Schwartz & Millar, 1996) and can positively affect achievement, most classrooms are devoid of these types of questions as a regular part of learning (Gallagher; Patterson, 1973). In reality, "there are many classrooms in which teachers rarely pose questions above the 'read–it–and–repeat–it' level" (Wolf, p. 1). Parker noted that most classrooms engender factual, convergent thinking questions; divergent thinking is a nontraditional concept and occurs infrequently in most classrooms.

To prepare gifted students for leadership roles and success in the workplace, educators must help them learn to generate alternatives in solving real-world problems by regularly incorporating divergent questions. Guilford's (1967) Structure of the Intellect distinguishes divergent and convergent thinking. The former is the ability to discover many potential answers or solutions to a problem, and the latter is defined as the ability to find the single best solution to a given problem.

Maker and Nielson (1996) advised teachers of the gifted to incorporate questioning strategies so that students will learn how to explain, elaborate, or clarify their often abstract ideas. Likewise, Daniels (1997) noted that curiosity is a common characteristic among gifted students, and helping them channel that instinct through questioning can stimulate them to want to investigate further answers to their curiosities. Asking simple, convergent thinking questions that require little thinking beyond knowledge recall does not foster growth of higher level thinking, which is critical in meeting the intellectual needs of gifted learners (Letzter, 1982).

In order to help students grow through the use of questioning, a teacher must first ensure that a safe, nonthreatening, encouraging, mutually respectful environment is established in the classroom (Feldhusen, 1994; Gallagher, 1985; Letzter, 1982; Maker & Nielson, 1996; Strasser, 1967).

Hunkins (1976) noted that one of the major factors in creating a supportive classroom climate for both teacher and student questioning is freedom. Students must feel the freedom to pose cognitive and affective questions at any time during learning, which will support the student in taking risks in processing ideas and questions and in formulating meaningful responses.

In order to provide such an atmosphere, respect is a central component of learning, whereby the teacher respects the ideas of the students and demonstrates this respect through active listening. Rather than formulating a quick answer or thinking of another question to pose students while a student is thinking through a question aloud, the teacher can model respect by listening to the ideas presented and reflecting upon his or her response prior to answering. Such a strategy shows the speaker the value of his or her ideas, promotes a safe environment for risk taking in conjecture, and illustrates that processing time may need to occur before a solution or response can be formulated. The teacher should also expect that all students will be active listeners, refraining from interrupting or distracting others while a speaker has the floor.

The role of the teacher as a responsive facilitator of learning is critical in this process. Not only should the teacher be responsive as a listener, but he or she should also provide necessary instruction to students in how to develop and pose questions, how to engage with others when thinking aloud, and how to provide encouragement and support to students and peers as they grapple with ideas. Additionally, the educator may need to provide data or other materials to assist in the thinking process or allow students needed time to access such resources and prepare for discussion (Hunkins, 1976). Teachers should monitor their classrooms to determine if an appropriate climate has been created to foster open inquiry among students. Hunkins provided a list of suggestions for evaluating one's teaching to determine if appropriate assistance has been offered to students (see Figure 1).

Strasser (1967) found that the learning environment is strongly affected by the teacher's behavior during his or her use of questioning. In addition to the concept of respect, Strasser advocated some ground rules for teachers to follow:

- Probe beyond simple, convenient, yes/no questions.

- Consider the specificity or vagueness of the questions and purpose.

- Divvy up summarizing and concluding responsibilities among students.

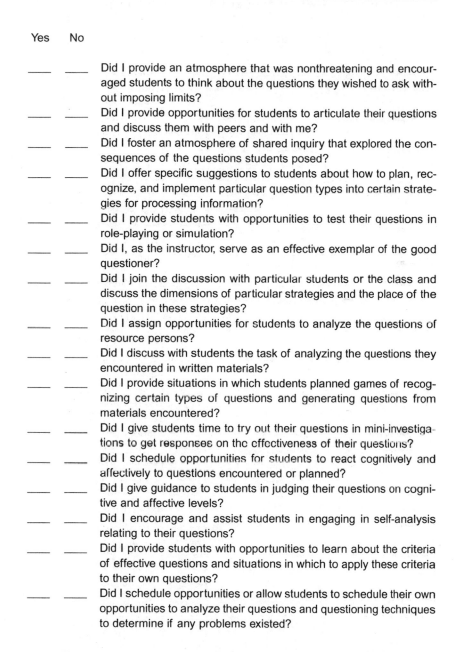

Yes   No

_____   _____   Did I provide an atmosphere that was nonthreatening and encouraged students to think about the questions they wished to ask without imposing limits?

_____   _____   Did I provide opportunities for students to articulate their questions and discuss them with peers and with me?

_____   _____   Did I foster an atmosphere of shared inquiry that explored the consequences of the questions students posed?

_____   _____   Did I offer specific suggestions to students about how to plan, recognize, and implement particular question types into certain strategies for processing information?

_____   _____   Did I provide students with opportunities to test their questions in role-playing or simulation?

_____   _____   Did I, as the instructor, serve as an effective exemplar of the good questioner?

_____   _____   Did I join the discussion with particular students or the class and discuss the dimensions of particular strategies and the place of the question in these strategies?

_____   _____   Did I assign opportunities for students to analyze the questions of resource persons?

_____   _____   Did I discuss with students the task of analyzing the questions they encountered in written materials?

_____   _____   Did I provide situations in which students planned games of recognizing certain types of questions and generating questions from materials encountered?

_____   _____   Did I give students time to try out their questions in mini-investigations to get responses on the effectiveness of their questions?

_____   _____   Did I schedule opportunities for students to react cognitively and affectively to questions encountered or planned?

_____   _____   Did I give guidance to students in judging their questions on cognitive and affective levels?

_____   _____   Did I encourage and assist students in engaging in self-analysis relating to their questions?

_____   _____   Did I provide students with opportunities to learn about the criteria of effective questions and situations in which to apply these criteria to their own questions?

_____   _____   Did I schedule opportunities or allow students to schedule their own opportunities to analyze their questions and questioning techniques to determine if any problems existed?

Figure 1. Teacher checklist for classroom atmosphere

Note. Adapted from *Involving Students in Questioning* (pp. 11–12), by P. Hunkins, 1976, Boston: Allyn and Bacon. Copyright ©1976 by Allyn and Bacon.

- Respond to student responses in an encouraging way.

- Wait for responses to questions with adequate student think time given.

- Pose a variety of types of questions.

- Address students by name during questioning.

- Avoid judgments, criticism, and condescension (pp. 207–209).

Tone of voice, facial expression, body language, and other nonverbal cues must foster an inviting and stimulating atmosphere that encourages risk taking through divergent thinking. Creating a student-friendly environment is essential to the success of an inquiry-based class. Therefore, teacher-student relationships must be of a supportive and respectful nature.

Maker and Nielson (1996) urged teachers and students to form open relationships to create an atmosphere appropriate for the investigation of challenging ideas through purposeful, well-timed questions asked by both teacher and students. A key to recognizing whether this climate has been established is how the student reacts to the line of inquiry. Defensive responses indicate that mutual respect and openness have not been established, in which case the teacher must continue to develop the environment and make it less threatening to the student.

Teacher reaction is also of importance, as the reaction should be appropriate to the purpose of the question. To continue development of student responses, teachers should avoid "canned" reactions to student responses, which may send messages to students that devalue their input. Conversely, careful attention to when and how the teacher responds can send students messages that their ideas are worthwhile, significant, pertinent, or sincere (see Figure 2). If the purpose of a line of questioning is to generate many student responses (i.e., brain-

Acceptable Responses	"Canned Responses"
Yes, I can understand that.	Yes.
I see what you mean.	I see.
I hadn't thought of that before.	Okay.
That makes a lot of sense.	Fine.

Figure 2. Teacher responses to student messages

Note. From *Curriculum Development and Teaching Strategies for Gifted Learners* (p. 48), by C. J. Maker & A. Nielson, 1996, Austin, TX: PRO-ED. Copyright ©1996 by PRO-ED. Reprinted with permission.

storming responses to a question) teachers should be careful not to evaluate and to defer judgment. A response from the teacher that indicates a "right" answer undermines the open climate established for generating ideas because it suggests that the teacher had a preconceived response, which should not occur in this type of activity and could inhibit future student participation and limit thinking (Maker & Nielson, 1996; Strasser, 1967).

Designing Appropriate Questions

Hyman (1979) recommended that teachers develop a plan of action for strategic questioning. Educators should understand why they are asking particular questions so that the intended student outcome is considered when designing the questions. Because student-teacher interaction is so complex and unpredictable, preliminary planning for a discussion or lesson is desirable; however, no teacher should attempt to map out exactly which questions to pose at any specific moment. Rather, the teacher should be cognizant of the learning occurring, where the learning is headed based on student interaction, and how a specifically posed question may alter, enrich, or extend the situation. Thus, knowing when and why to ask the appropriate question is a skill to be honed by the teacher. Hyman recommended that teachers employ specific strategies when asking questions (see Figure 3).

Strategy	Description	Suggestions	Examples	
Mixed	Teachers intentionally mix the types of questions asked, avoiding the same type of questioning and providing a mixture of both cognitive variations and types.	Recognize that there are types of cognitive processes.	1.Definitional (giving meaning) 2. Empirical (give responses based upon perceptions or observations) 3. Evaluative (value judgment) 4. Metaphysical (moral/ethical)	1. What is nonviolent conflict? 2. Is the world becoming more tolerant of different cultures? 3. Should the legal driving age be raised? 4. Should humans strive for world peace, or is it human nature to have conflict?
		Type of questioning production (3 types)	• Yes/no questions • Selection of responses (do you prefer Shakespeare or Melville?) • Construction (Give your opinion of the ending of this novel).	
Peaks	Pose a question to a student and continue to probe with related questioning and then move to another student.	Progress from simple (knowledge or fact questions) to more complex questions (conclusions, evaluations).	1. When was the Vietnam War? (factual) 2. Compare Vietnam with Desert Storm. (comparison) 3. What caused Vietnam? (causes) 4. What conclusions about our government can you draw based upon your understanding of Vietnam? (conclusions, generalizations, inference from facts)	
Plateaus	The instructor asks a battery of questions of the same type to four students before moving on to the next level of questioning to the same four students.	This strategy allows for a multitude of responses at each questioning level until sufficient discussion has been achieved, perhaps employing a probing question.	A. Sam, what is one of the rights in the Bill of Rights? B. Glen, what is another right? C. Karen, have you thought of another right? D. Robert, what is another right that has not been listed?	
		Then the instructor moves on to a more difficult level of questioning with the same students.	A. Sam, what is the purpose of the right you named? B. Glen, explain the purpose of the third right. C. Karen, what was the purpose of the right to bear arms? D. Robert, what is the purpose of the right to a fair trial?	

Figure 3. General strategies for asking questions

Note. Adapted from *Strategic Questioning,* by R. Hyman, 1979, Englewood Cliffs, NJ: Prentice Hall. Copyright ©1979 by Prentice Hall. Adapted with permission.

Types of Questions

There are several types of questions teachers can use to stimulate creative, critical, and higher level thinking. The most commonly recommended is the divergent thinking question that probes beyond the convergent, one-correct-answer question, thus allowing students to delve more deeply into an idea. These questions generally follow the open-ended format that allows for purposeful, student-centered discussion (Grambo, 1997; Letzter, 1982; Pollack, 1988). Letzter felt that "teacher questions should be broad or open so that students will be free to respond with their own thoughts. . . . [And] if this line of questioning is handled well, the students move forward in their own analysis of . . . problems and topics" (p. 195). Although the use of "open-ended questions may be somewhat threatening to the teacher because of the lack of guidelines in evaluating children's responses," teachers should still strive to find meaningful and purposeful opportunities regularly for this line of inquiry. The goal is to foster a learning environment that values the process of learning to arrive at answers, rather than just the answers themselves (Pollack, p. 4).

Additional types of questions, including interpretation, comparison-analysis, synthesis, evaluation, sensitivity to problems, and clarifying problems, are provocative and hypothetical in nature. They encourage thoughtful reading, listening, and viewing and ask students to see new relationships (Feldhusen, 1994). Teachers must be aware of the intended processes they want their students to use when structuring their questions. Hence, Feldhusen recommended various types of questions to elicit different "types of thinking processes: memory/cognition, convergent, divergent, and evaluation" (p. 173). Similarly, teachers must recognize which situations call for follow-up (Maker & Nielson, 1996).

Heuristic Strategies

Heuristic strategies are ideal tools for developing creative ideas (Callahan, 1978). Among these strategies is attribute listing, or using questions to stimulate the generation of ideas to improve or change something, then suggesting how to implement the changes. Attribute listing involves generating a list of the qualities, parts, properties, or elements of a given object. Attributes of a car would include the engine, tires, body, frame, interior fabric, seats, and lights.

Morphological analysis, which is similar to attribute listing, involves creating a new product by combining components in a new way (Manktelow, 2003). Each of the aforementioned car attributes would be placed at the top of a column in a matrix, and below each heading variations on these topics would be listed to encourage students to consider multiple dimensions of a problem and possible solutions. For both attribute listing and morphological analysis, Callahan included a list of questions to be used during brainstorming to stimulate students' thinking (see Figure 4).

Callahan's strategy is similar to Eberle's SCAMPER model (Glenn, 1997), which also fosters creativity through divergence, intuition, originality, and imagination. The SCAMPER

Other uses	Can it be put to use as is?
Adaptation	What else is like it?
Modification	What new twist could be made?
Magnification	What could be added?
Minification	What could be omitted?
Substitution	What else can do it?
Rearrangement	Can you use a different sequence?
Reversibility	Can you do the opposite?
Combination	Can items be blended?
Transformation	Can you change its form in any way?

Figure 4. Callahan's questioning

Note. Adapted from *Developing Creativity in the Gifted and Talented* (pp. 30–31), by C. Callahan, 1978, Reston, VA: Council for Exceptional Children. Copyright ©1978 by Council for Exceptional Children.

model also allows students to brainstorm an object or idea and its alternatives (see Figure 5). For example, students may consider how a cellular phone may be improved or altered to realize potential new uses and markets. What could be substituted for the cell phone? Perhaps a radio, handheld digital portfolio, television, or video camera. How could this product be combined with others? Perhaps with a fax machine, portable scanner, digital positioning system, or computer. Students would consider each of the SCAMPER elements in reengineering possibilities for the cell phone.

Interpretive Questions

Interpretive questions also challenge students to think critically (Wolf, 1997). Rather than filling in missing information or altering a set of solutions to fit alternatives, "interpretive questions propose that [students] understand the consequences for information or ideas" (Wolf, p. 3). For example, an art teacher may ask a student to examine a portrait and consider

Thinking Process	Purpose of Process
Substitute	An object or person takes the place of another.
Combine	Items are united, perhaps to improve a product.
Adapt	Alterations are made to convert the use of the object for a particular function or need.
Modify/magnify/minify	The form is enlarged or reduced in size or shape, prompting consideration of other uses or needs based upon length, weight, density, speed, height, scope.
Put to other uses	An object is reconsidered for its function.
Eliminate	An object is reconceived without a facet or dimension initially included. Evaluation of how the product may be more useful or alternately useful in this state is involved.
Reverse or rearrange	Variations on the layout, vision, or concept of the idea or object are considered to see how the product might be used for other purposes or may be improved based on this change.

Figure 5. SCAMPER

Note. From *Scamper,* by B. Eberle, 1995, Waco, TX: Prufrock Press. Copyright ©1995 by Prufrock Press. Reprinted with permission.

- Examine your work on this project and discuss how you've grown as a writer.

- Discuss your attitude toward this activity and how it may be different from other activities we've done in English.

- As you look back at your goals for this semester, examine and discuss which you were able to achieve and which you were not able to achieve. Consider why some were or were not attainable and how your choices this semester affected your achievement of these goals.

Figure 6. Reflective questions

how the elimination of a certain object might change the image (Wolf). Interpretive questions also ask students to consider how changes would affect a situation, such as considering how their lives might be different if they don't attend college or if they choose to get married at a young age.

Reflective Questions

Reflective questions (see Figure 6) encourage students to consider their thinking processes and examine their strategies in a metacognitive fashion. By posing questions during and after learning, teachers can "debrief" students, which can bolster future efforts (Maker & Nielson, 1996). Meaningful idea exchanges during class discussions can occur by using reflective thinking and questioning, during which time the teacher must carefully plan what sort of follow-up questions to ask students in order to clarify murky ideas (Will, 1987).

Reflective questions are also a way to stimulate conversation and the examination of basic assumptions (Wolf, 1997). Students must learn to consider how and why their thinking is so and what has led them to their conclusions. In this manner, the teacher focuses learning on the investigation of student ideas to bring about further discussion and turns student statements around into questions that challenge them to think more deeply about their own thinking (Letzter, 1982).

Questioning the Validity and Reliability of Information

Gallagher and Gallagher (1994) recommended that educators pose questions to students so they learn to evaluate sources accurately. At this time of heightened information access through technology, students may easily become distracted with the aesthetic nuances of the Internet and overlook the credibility and reliability of sources.

The PROP method, developed by O'Reilly (as cited in Gallagher & Gallagher, 1994), provides students a method for analyzing conflicting information. Students should consider whether the source is primary or secondary (P), whether the source had reason to distort information (R), whether other evidence exists to support the statements within a document (O), and whether the information within a document was rendered as a public or private statement (P), which could alter the purpose of the statement and why such information was provided.

Through questioning these facets of information, students learn to become more discriminating consumers of information as children, which may ultimately impact later decision-making skills in their future personal and professional lives.

Models for Questioning

Several models have been developed that shape education's use of questioning. From the ancient Greeks, education has adopted the traditions of Socrates as a facilitator of learning through probing questions and the search for truth. The Junior Great Books Program, for example, is designed around Socratic questioning. A more modern contributor, Benjamin Bloom, has also greatly impacted how teachers structure learning through the levels of cognition. More recent work, particularly that of Winocur and Maurer (1997), as well as de Bono (1999), provides suggestions for thinking strategies. In these strategic thinking models, positive outcomes for students have been found when such strategic plans for critical thinking are employed, including the purposeful questioning of students.

A review of the models and thinking strategies generated by these leaders is provided to assist teachers of the gifted in designing appropriate instructional challenges for gifted students.

Bloom's Taxonomy

Bloom's taxonomy, initially published in the mid-1950s, has served as a seminal guide for educators in constructing appropriate cognitive challenges for students of all ability levels. Due to the abilities and needs of gifted students, teachers of the gifted are encouraged to design learning challenges focused less on the lower cognitive objectives, such as knowledge and comprehension, and more upon the higher level thinking skills needed in the upper ranges of the taxonomy, such as analysis, application, and evaluation. Likewise, questioning strategies for the gifted should follow this recommendation, whereby teachers and students engage in questioning at the higher levels. To become skilled in the art of effective questioning, teachers can look to Bloom's taxonomy (see Figure 7) to gauge their proficiency and target areas for growth as questioners.

Gallagher (1985), Patterson (1973), Pollack (1988) and Wolf (1997) have stressed the examination of Bloom's taxonomy to see how to structure questions at each level, focusing on the application, analysis, synthesis, and evaluation levels as higher level planes for gifted students (see Figure 8).

Teachers can utilize the list of questions as they develop their lessons. The questions may be sequenced in the order presented in Figure 7, or they may be included in the order that is most appropriate for the lesson at hand. Reflective questions, due to their metacognitive function, may also work well as closing questions or culminating questions in a discussion or at the end of a unit of study.

Students should have the opportunity to share their responses to these questions with each other in pairs, small groups, whole-class discussions, or in conference with the teacher. Furthermore, students should be encouraged to develop their own questions at these levels in order to investigate issues of importance to them in the classroom and beyond.

Gallagher and Gallagher (1994) also suggested that teachers note the precepts of Guilford's Structure of the Intellect in

Objective	Descriptors of Action Verbs for Each
Knowledge	list, define, tell, describe, identify, show, label, collect, examine, tabulate, quote, name
Comprehension	summarize, describe, interpret, contrast, predict, associate, distinguish, estimate, differentiate, discuss, extend
Application	apply, demonstrate, calculate, complete, illustrate, show, solve, examine, modify, relate, change, classify, experiment, discover
Analysis	analyze, separate, order, explain, connect, classify, arrange, divide, compare, select, explain, infer
Synthesis	combine, integrate, modify, rearrange, substitute, plan, create, design, invent, what if?, compose, formulate, prepare, generalize, rewrite
Evaluation	assess, decide, rank, grade, test, measure, recommend, convince, select, judge, explain, discriminate, support, conclude, compare, summarize

**Figure 7. Bloom's Taxonomy of Educational Objectives
in the Cognitive Domain**

Note. Adapted from *Taxonomy of Educational Objectives: The Classification of Educational Goals. Handbook I: Cognitive Domain*, by B. S. Bloom (Ed.), 1956, New York: Longmans, Green. Copyright ©1956 Longmans, Green. Adapted with permission.

planning for higher level thinking; the types of questions in this model range from lower level memory questions to questions promoting cognition, divergent thinking, and ultimately convergent thinking.

Inference Questions	• What do you know by looking at this photograph? (asks the photography teacher) • What do you know about the character in this selection? • In which era might this have been written? What contextual clues indicate this?
Interpretation Questions	• How do the descriptions of characters in The Scarlet Letter reveal the author's tones? • How would the music be different if it were played in a major key, rather than a minor key? • How would the artwork be different if produced in glass, rather than plastic?
Transfer Questions	• How would Locke have written about this political scandal? • How would a modern-day musician interpret this classical piece? • How would Gandhi have suggested this conflict be resolved?
Questions About Hypotheses	• How might history have been different if Lincoln had never delivered the Gettysburg Address? • Based on current social and political issues, what do you think future movies, novels, and plays will be about? • How would culture be different if Shakespeare's works had not reached prominence?
Reflective Questions	• What about this concept do I still not know? • What about my work has improved? Needs improvement? • Where does my work reflect my understanding of this concept? • What does this work say about me?

Figure 8. Range of questions

Note. Adapted from "The Art of Questioning" by D. Wolf, 1987, *Academic Connections*, Winter, p. 3. Retrieved May 25, 2004, from http://www.exploratorium.com/IFI/resources/workshops/artofquestioning.html. Copyright ©1987 by College Entrance Examination Board.

In addition to questions in the cognitive domain, educators are encouraged to pose questions within the affective domain (Krathwohl, Bloom, & Masia, 1964; see Figures 9 and 10). While the cognitive and affective domains were not meant to be separated in teaching, identifying the types of affective questions to be posed that may be a part of the learning process encourages students to think about their value systems as they process information in the cognitive domain.

Junior Great Books

One of the most successful and frequently mentioned questioning models emanates from the Junior Great Books (JGB) program, which follows a reading and discussion format in which a teacher leads discussions through questions (see Figure 11). The Junior Great Books Program is based upon the Socratic seminar model, where student participants convene in a circle and discuss a shared reading guided by the "teacher's open-ended, provocative questions" (Ball & Brewer, 2000, p. 1), engaging primarily in discussing the selected text with each other, rather than the teacher, who serves as a facilitator or guide, eliciting clarification or extension of ideas from students.

Based upon the practices of Socrates, who posed questions to his students to encourage truth seeking and self-awareness without providing his answers, this model has been successful in engaging students in class discussions because it allows them the opportunity to build a learning community within their class. Students are engaged in a social relationship with each other as they explore the complexities of the reading or issue at hand. The connections forged during the Socratic seminar allow students to relate prior discussions or readings to new ideas or concepts unearthed during discussion, fostering greater retention of information.

Students also become more skilled in speaking and listening, skills often overlooked in traditional teacher-centered classrooms where instructors dominate classes with lectures, leaving few opportunities for student voices or meaningful

Level	Subcategories
Receiving (attending)	Awareness Willingness to receive Controlled or selected attention
Responding	Acquiescence in responding Willingness to respond Satisfaction in response
Valuing	Acceptance of a value Preference for a value Commitment
Organization	Conceptualization of a value Organization of a value system
Characterization by a value or value complex	Generalized set Characterization

Figure 9. Questions in the affective domain

Note. Adapted from *Involving Students in Questioning*, by P. Hunkins, 1976, Boston: Allyn and Bacon. Copyright ©1976 by Allyn and Bacon.

exchanges between students. Probably the most dynamic aspect of the Socratic seminar is the sense of control that is bestowed upon students as they grapple with ideas. Students also learn to sharpen their skills in constructive criticism, learning to share opposing viewpoints without attacking the ideas of others. Furthermore, students learn to provide logical ideas to support their views, and they develop a critical ear for detecting the absence of logic in the reasoning of others or perhaps themselves. While the teacher may still guide the pace, questioning, and textual choices of the seminar, students control the ideas and talk time, which should ideally occur during a 90–minute

Level	Key Phrases	Examples of Questions
Receiving (attending)	Are you aware Do you know Have you heard Do you recognize Will you accept Are you interested Would you like	• Among these pictures of famous art works, do you recognize any? • Indicate which of these art works you'd like to know more about. • Other students have indicated that they would like to have more learning experiences in literature that are tied to the humanities, including learning about art works and their creators. Are you also interested in these experiences?
Responding	Record how Have you contributed Indicate which Do you observe	• Of the following choices, indicate which you would prefer to do at home rather than in school: journaling, editing, or reading. • William James indicates that people act differently depending upon whose company they are in. Do you agree with this sentiment, disagree, or are you somewhere in between? • View this photograph and record how you feel while viewing it.
Valuing	Do you feel responsible for List which Defend your stance Are you loyal to Rank order Do you participate actively	• In Macbeth, which character seemed the most reprehensible to you? • If you could spend 30 minutes with any American President living or deceased, who would be your top choice? • Identify how you might have shifted "selves" while you were with certain people this week.
Organ-ization	In your opinion As you view Please explain Have you weighed alternatives Does the statement imply In your own words	• Based upon the film we have just viewed, please explain which behaviors of the main character you find honorable and which you feel are dishonorable. • As you view our country's participation in recent foreign affairs, is it your opinion that our country is acting in keeping with the highest moral ideals?
Character-ization by a value or value complex	Are you confident What would you do How do you feel Is that your philosophy Indicate those	• A new student who is from a Spanish-speaking country will become a member of our class next week. How will you help this student adjust to our class? • Of the following life goals, indicate which you strive to incorporate in your life.

Figure 10. Affective domain question phrases and examples

Note. Adapted from *Involving Students in Questioning*, by P. Hunkins, 1976, Boston: Allyn and Bacon. Copyright ©1976 by Allyn and Bacon.

Factual questions	• Who?
	• Where?
	• When?
Evaluative questions	• What do you think about this story?
	• Do you disagree or agree with . . . ?
	• Would you have made the same decision in these circumstances?
	• Have you ever experienced the character's feelings? When?
	• What did you think this story was going to be about?
	• What do you think about the ending?
Interpretive questions	• Can you support your opinion with a reference to the text?
	• Where else in the passage does the author also suggest that . . . ?
	• According to the author of this passage, should . . . ?

Figure 11. Junior Great Books

Note. From *Instructional Strategies for Teaching the Gifted* (pp. 192–193), by J. Parker, 1989, Boston: Allyn and Bacon. Copyright ©1989 by Allyn and Bacon.

block period for extended thinking and discussion. During those 90 minutes, students dominate the discussion through exchanging ideas and responding to those of their peers.

Parker (1989) cited the JGB program and the Great Books program as ideal models for using questioning techniques through "shared inquiry, a qualitatively different approach to the teaching of literature, [which] is extremely well-suited for use with gifted readers" (p. 192). The JGB program uses three types of questions: factual, evaluative, and interpretive (see Figure 11). Factual questions are convergent questions that can be answered "directly from information supplied in the story" (Parker, p. 192). The answers are not debatable. Evaluative questions ask students to consider their personal experiences and attitude. The question relies on the students' knowledge of the story, but they need not refer directly to the story to respond. Interpretive questions, the type emphasized and used the most in the JGB program, require divergent thinking by "using the reader's intuitive powers and information from the story" (Parker, p. 192).

The program has guidelines for conducting discussions, beginning with teacher-developed clusters of basic, interpretive questions to generate debatable discussion among students. It then moves to follow-up questions that ask students to explore implications of the basic questions, support a response, correct a factual error, elicit additional responses or opinions, encourage discussion, clarify a statement, develop the most important idea in a response, encourage a participant to examine his or her response, or return a discussion to the reading (Parker, 1989, p. 193). Since this is a challenging program to initiate, JGB offers beginning and advanced workshops to help teachers gain competency in these techniques.

For educators new to the Socratic seminar, framing questions for discussion can be one of the most challenging aspects of this strategy. Ball and Brewer (2000) recommended that the teacher follow specific guidelines in developing purposeful questions for discussion. First, the teacher should read the selection or text carefully, noting meaningful quotations and listing the issues that should be addressed in discussion. This list is then used as the basis of the development of questions for the seminar. Ball and Brewer suggested developing three types of questions: opening, core, and closing.

Opening questions are broad and should be the initial questions posed to students. The purpose of the opening question is to allow students to connect to the questions from a multitude of places within the reading that provide evidence for a response. These questions may elicit a variety of responses from students and may sustain discussion from 15 to 45 minutes of class, depending upon the sophistication of the students or the length and complexity of the reading. Teachers should avoid developing opening questions that may result in "yes" or "no" responses; rather, they should focus on crafting questions that are engaging, insightful, and compelling, thus sending readers back to the text for support for their responses. Teachers should also avoid judgment statements in these opening questions that might indicate his or her values or position. Ball and Brewer underscored the importance of the teacher as a neutral participant in the construction and delivery of the question, which includes both verbal and nonverbal gestures in communicating the questions in order to foster an open, inviting discussion. Furthermore, teachers should consider the language used in communicating ideas. Whenever possible, the facilitator should avoid developing questions that are "sterile or fancy" (Ball & Brewer, p. 63). Rather than asking "What are the major character flaws of Macbeth?," (in which "character flaws" is a teacher word), try asking "What's up with this Macbeth guy?," which is more colloquial and less threatening to students and is broad enough to foster responses and be supported by evidence from a variety of places within the text.

Core questions are more focused than opening questions and should thus encompass less discussion time. Ball and Brewer (2000) suggested including three to eight core questions during discussion, depending upon the complexity and length of the reading. Specific quotes or lines from the selection may be targeted for discussion/analysis/interpretation. The question may begin with "What does [the speaker, character, author] mean by [insert quote here]?" Teachers should provide the location in the text to assist students in comprehending the question and providing visual support for students who are not as skilled in listening. Other core questions may begin with "how" or "why." The teacher must listen carefully to students' responses and shape follow-up questions based upon the ideas presented. If a student only partially responds to a question, the teacher could build upon the student's ideas in reframing the question: "Let's consider Sam's idea . . ." or "Sam mentioned that . . . Are you implying, then, Sam, that . . . ?" This type of refocusing or reframing of questions allows students to continue to think about their ideas. By focusing on a student idea in moving the discussion forward, the teacher adds to the sense of student control and empowerment that are hallmarks of Socratic seminars.

In developing a closing question for the discussion, teachers should strive to connect an issue from the selection with the experiences of the students (Ball & Brewer, 2000). One such question, based upon Martin Luther King, Jr.'s "I Have a Dream" speech is "Do you see in your daily experiences that King's vision of a less violent society has emerged?" This question relates a concept of nonviolent protest within the personal context of the students' lives. Personalizing the closing question is central in connecting to the students, so educators should include "you" or "we" in these questions (Ball & Brewer, p. 65).

Teachers are also encouraged to develop questions that are applicable to all students. Ball and Brewer (2000) noted that, in a closing discussion of the Gettysburg Address, teachers should avoid asking "For what are you willing to give your 'last full measure of devotion?'" or "For what are you willing to die?" because such questions presuppose that all students are willing to die for something. This excludes those who may not have such feelings or beliefs from relating to the question. Rather, the facilitator may ask "In our society, what are people willing to die for?" (p. 65).

Teachers are also encouraged to use follow-up questions in probing student responses (see Figure 12). While it is desirable for the teacher to pose only one opening and one closing question, with students actively and meaningfully engaging with each other throughout the seminar, occasionally the teacher may have to probe student thinking to clarify faulty logic or muddled connections. The teacher may also recognize oppor-

THE PRACTICAL STRATEGIES SERIES IN GIFTED EDUCATION   33

Student Behavior	Teacher Response
Offers an opinion without evidence from the selection	"Where in the text can you find support for your opinion?"
Vague, unclear explanation for reasoning offered	"What do you mean by [restate vague phrase]?"
Provides a long explanation	"Are you saying that [puts student idea in a concise statement]?"
Heads down wrong path	"How can you support that with evidence from the text?" or "Does anyone disagree with this point of view? Why?"
Engages in circular thinking, arriving nowhere	"Can you rethink your ideas and offer a point?"
Makes a generalization	"Why do you say that?"

Figure 12. Follow-up questions

Note. Adapted from *Socratic Seminars in the Block*, by W. Ball & P. Brewer, 2000, Larchmont, NY: Eye on Education. Copyright ©2000 by Eye on Education. Reprinted with permission.

tunities to push students to think with more academic rigor.

However, the teacher should avoid invoking follow-up questions unnecessarily, as they may lead to intimidation or the perception that students don't own the conversation. To avoid the need to pose follow-up questions, educators should clearly indicate their expectations of students prior to the seminar, giving special emphasis to the need for reasoned responses that are verified or supported with evidence from the text and avoiding pitfalls to unsound thinking such as "generalizations, circular thinking, faulty logic, or unsubstantiated thinking" (Ball &

Brewer, 2000, p. 66). The seminar can be a powerful, engaging, motivating experience for students and the teacher if students are allowed the freedom to explore challenging ideas and issues related to a text known to all participants, so long as students understand the format and their roles as speakers and listeners.

IMPACT

IMPACT (Increase Maximal Performance by Activating Critical Thinking) is a comprehensive program designed for teachers of the gifted to use across the curriculum by developing students' abilities to transfer thinking skills and gain competency in the use of thinking tools to realize increased achievement (see Figure 13). Through the use of open-ended questions, students enhance their thinking abilities. In one school, the principal reported an elevated cognitive level of engagement due to the ongoing nature of the students' reflections about their thinking processes in the IMPACT program (Winocur & Maurer, 1997).

IMPACT is a strategy that can assist students in developing systematic thinking skills for use across disciplines and for various purposes (Winocur & Maurer, 1997). At the core of IMPACT is critical thinking, and teachers are trained to provide specific behaviors that will foster the development of crit-

Enabling Skills	Perceiving	Observing
		Comparing/Contrasting
	Conceiving	Grouping/Labeling
		Classifying/categorizing
	Seriating	Ordering
		Sequencing
		Patterning
		Prioritizing
Processes	Analyzing	Fact/Opinion
		Relevant/Irrelevant Information
		Reliable/Unreliable Sources
	Questioning	Inferring
		Meaning of Statements
		Cause-Effect Relationships
		Generalizations
		Predictions
		Assumptions
		Point of View
Operations	Logical Reasoning	Inductive
		Deductive
	Evaluation	Judgment
		Decision Making

Figure 13. IMPACT: Universe of critical thinking skills

Note. Adapted from "Critical Thinking and Gifted Students: Using IMPACT to Improve Teaching and Learning" (pp. 308–317), by S. Winocur & P. Maurer, in N. Colangelo & G. A. Davis (Eds.), *Handbook of Gifted Education* (2nd ed.), 1997, Boston: Allyn and Bacon. Copyright ©1997 by Allyn and Bacon. Reprinted with permission.

ical thinking in their classrooms. Among these behaviors are cooperative learning interactions, sequencing skills from lower level to higher level cognitive challenges, sequencing concepts from concrete to abstract modes, demonstrating effective thinking and behaviors, questioning techniques to foster higher level cognitive functioning, prompting or cuing thinking, posing appropriate follow-up questions, utilizing graphic organizers, incorporating appropriate wait time during questioning, and teaching so that concepts and skills are transferred from one subject or situation to another.

In addition to assisting educators in altering their behaviors to improve student learning, IMPACT also provides teachers with specific lesson planning design to assist in eliciting sound thinking from students: teaching of thinking, teaching for thinking, and teaching about thinking, which are three essential components to building better critical thinking skills in students (Winocur & Maurer, 1997). Through IMPACT, teachers learn how to provide direct instruction in how to solve problems and think through situations, how to create stimulating and supportive classroom climates that foster critical thinking, and how to engage students in metacognitive discussion that challenge them to evaluate the quality of their thinking.

Utilizing skills, processes, and operations (see Figure 13), students are challenged to move toward improved critical thinking skills. However, unlike programs that are abstract in nature, IMPACT provides guides for teachers to show students how to think in concrete terms and then advance toward higher levels of abstraction as concepts in thinking are mastered. In this manner, educators may differentiate instruction for students based upon their skills, processes, or operational levels, developing lessons that operate on a continuum of concrete to abstract levels based upon the individual needs of the students. Students may be grouped according to level of critical thinking skill understanding and complexity, performance on specific tasks within academic disciplines and how well they transfer concepts from one discipline to another, or how well they assimilate the skill within one domain to another.

Evidence for the success of the IMPACT model was established through training and demonstration with a school district in Texas with a diversity of students from African American, Hispanic, and Caucasian families. Within this district, 33% of students received free and reduced lunches, 8% were served in a program for students with learning disabilities, and 8% were served in a program for students with gifts and talents. Prior to the in-service in IMPACT, one third of the students in the school had not passed a state mathematics test; following the training, the passing rate dramatically increased in reading, math, and the entire state assessment battery. Although specific information about the performance of gifted students is not provided, the authors indicated that the instruction of the gifted in the regular classroom was important to their growth as critical thinkers, and opportunities for continued development in this area were increased as a result of the IMPACT training (Winocur & Maurer, 1997).

Thinking Hats

Edward de Bono (1970) advocated the "Why?" technique, whereby students are encouraged to challenge assumptions through lateral thinking. This strategy is intended to create a "discomfort with any explanation"; hence, learners grow through attempting to view concepts differently by reconstructing the pattern of thinking and perceiving. Ultimately, the goal is for students to challenge assumed boundaries by asking, "Why?" (de Bono, p. 102).

To foster thinking beyond traditional pro/con limitations, de Bono developed a method for groups or individuals to examine issues, ideas, concepts, and challenges through a broader framework. Using the images of thinking hats, de Bono (1999) conceived of six hats with specific functions and corresponding colors for groups to examine a concept from multiple perspectives. The six hats method has been widely adopted in the corporate world on an international basis, as it has been recognized as an efficient strategy for problem solving. Educators can also find value in teaching students how to approach issues through a variety of lenses in order to consider fully all implications of a situation and find resolutions to a challenge.

de Bono's six hats (see Figure 14) are assigned a specific color and a specific mode of thinking. In creative thinking activities, all participants imagine wearing the same color hat and performing the same type of thinking, then proceed to another color to consider alternate thinking about a given topic. This strategy may be appropriate during a group action research project or service learning opportunity. During the latter, for example, students may be initiating a discussion of how to address the low voter turnout at school elections. Prior to developing a plan for addressing this concern, students may engage in examining the issues related to the problem through using the six hats strategy.

First, students would share their knowledge of the issue, such as how many students in the school have participated in elections during the last several years, who supplied these facts and figures, the reliability of the source, and whether more information is needed. The discussion would proceed to an examination of feelings about this issue, whether participants feel that it merits their continued attention, whether they feel they can make an impact, and what the feelings might be about this problem overall. The discussion would then follow a similar pattern as students follow the six thinking hats order to consider their selected issue from a variety of vantage points prior to moving forward with a plan of action.

de Bono (1999) recommended that groups initiate discussion by asking all participants to consider the facts and figures of a given topic. This type of idea generation, known as "white hat thinking," encourages individuals to avoid discussions pertaining to feelings, potential negative or positive consequences,

Hat Color	Corresponding Hat Function
White	Objective thinking about facts, figures, and information. Wearers consider the origin of the information and the comprehensiveness of the information and whether other information is needed or missing.
Red	Represents intuitive thoughts and feelings. Participants briefly discuss feelings associated with ideas, but do not investigate the origin of these feelings or the merit of these feelings. This hat allows for an immediate "gut check" from wearers.
Yellow	Wearers consider why particular suggestions may be viable, and what the possible outcomes and consequences may be. The reasoning behind each positive value statement is also discussed to support the suggested benefits of a concept or idea.
Black	Examinees consider why a solution or concept may not be workable, citing reasons to support this line of thinking. Participants examine the pitfalls, potential negative repercussions, and faults of the issue at hand.
Green	Creative thinking is explored at this juncture as all thinkers examine how to overcome or address the black hat concerns. Alternatives, new ideas, and possibilities are generated with the goal of overcoming the black hat issues and working toward preserving or solidifying the yellow hat concerns.
Blue	Management of the thinking occurs when wearers identify the focus of their plan, summarize the ideas and concepts generated, provide action plans for the intended outcomes, and move to a resolution.

Figure 14. Six thinking hats

Note. From *Six Thinking Hats,* by E. de Bono, 1999, Boston: Back Bay. Copyright ©1999 by Back Bay. Reprinted with permission.

and other issues. Within this white hat thinking level, participants may even delineate between known facts and believed facts. Known facts are verified immediately with available data, and believed facts are listed with the goal of later verification prior to moving to the next mode of thinking.

For example, in a student-centered discussion about the issue of the need for candy and soda machines at schools, students might list the known facts gathered prior to the discussion: monthly profits to the school and to the supplier during the last 5 years, allocation of these profits to programs within the school, what these allocations funded in previous years, caloric figures for items sold in machines, times machines are accessible to students, and cost of individual items in the machines. Believed facts may include the increase in child obesity at the school, reported opinions of parents and concerned citizens (but not the opinions of students, as this is a later hat), and believed relationships between purchases and health among students in the school. The key to this type of thinking is for students to consider facts early in discussions so that later thinking may be guided by verified facts and figures. Before moving to the next thinking hat, teachers should allow time for students to verify the believed facts generated.

Red hat thinking allows participants to voice opinions and feelings related to a concept without the requirement of justifying these feelings (de Bono, 1999). Students may introduce ideas with statements such as "I feel that . . ." or "My intuition indicates that . . ." Students can experience the opportunity to share the emotions and in the process learn that, while intuition frequently drives decision making, this strategy may not be well informed. Students may be allowed the opportunity to pass on sharing feelings at this stage, or they may report their mixed feelings about the subject, in which case the facilitator is encouraged to probe further to assist the student in uncovering the duality of his or her feelings. One caveat for participants to keep in mind is that red hat thinking is about the sharing of emotions—not judgments.

Another function of the red hat is to validate emotions, which are so often omitted from decision-making discussions. Students should have the opportunity to learn to voice their emotions without apology. They should learn that thinking about feelings is a part of an overall process and that these feelings are part of a complete picture (or map, to use de Bono's label) that will ultimately guide them in coming to a resolution. In red hat thinking about the soda/candy machine issue, students might volunteer feelings about the presence of the machine or its removal: "I feel good when I get a good grade and my teacher lets me go to the machine for a treat" or "It is my intuition that many of the students would be upset if the machines were removed."

Black hat thinking, which is most closely associated with critical thinking, allows participants to vocalize their views of how the issue at hand is wrong, potentially won't work, or is faulty based upon logic (de Bono, 1999). Discussants partici-pate in thinking cautiously about the given topic, considering the potential barriers, deficiencies in thinking, or problems with previously stated information. For example, if during white hat thinking a participant indicated an outdated fact or figure, later during black hat thinking, this criticism may be offered to help mold the relevance of the previously stated information. This type of statement would not have been pro-ductive or prudent during the collection of facts and figures, but at this stage, the critical analysis point, such a statement is desired. If it had been offered during the white hat stage, then other participants may have felt wary of offering ideas for fear of criticism. Such responses may have contributed to a limited sharing of ideas, which potentially would have been a less pro-ductive expenditure of time. Participants learn to withhold such critical analysis until the appropriate time during black hat thinking. For example, black hat thinking might result in a par-ticipant in the discussion of the vending machine issue suggest-ing that removal of the machines would result in fewer students having access to band instruments, which are funded through the proceeds from the candy machines.

Risk assessment is an essential part of black hat thinking (de Bono, 1999), and students can learn the importance of thinking through such risks if the teacher prompts responses to the following questions: "What would happen if that action were taken?" or "How might students or teachers react?" Students may respond with a variety of ideas, including "Healthier choices in machines might be a way to save the machines and continue to make money, but I doubt that students will spend as much money on fruit or water as they would on candy." While this type of thinking is most often used during the examination of an issue, it is important that it be situated within a larger context of all thinking types within this strategy for it to be effective and for students to grasp the limitations of relying on critical thinking only as part of decision making.

The yellow hat allows participants to examine the value within their thinking through examining the positive aspects of the ideas presented thus far. Learning to develop "value sensitivity" is a skill that many people rarely undertake (de Bono, 1999). The yellow hat allows discussants to examine logically how, to whom, and for what purposes ideas are valuable. This opportunity to examine the positives allows participants to develop the ability to see the good in things, an opportunity not often afforded most individuals. This opportunity may help to uncover previously unseen merits of a statement or idea.

For example, a student might suggest that "If vending machines are removed from our school, then we may have to find alternate ways of raising funds for our extracurricular activities; this might also lead to healthier lifestyles, less student absenteeism, and, in the long run, a healthier country with fewer high-cost medical bills, which could relieve the current burdens of the health care industry and our Medicaid system." However, not all yellow hat thinking may lead to fruitful findings, as participants, try as they might, may simply not be able to generate a positive idea about an issue, especially given the facts, feelings, and critical thinking already explored. This is understandable and acceptable, but the opportunity to discover the positives and justify these with logic should always be encouraged.

Green hat thinking allows students to examine alternatives to suggested ideas or options not previously offered (de Bono, 1999). Green was selected as the color of this hat to correspond to energy, growth, the stemming of ideas, and the generation of new ones. With green hat thinking, possibilities are offered and the opportunity for fresh thinking and creativity are given. For example, rather than removing the vending machines immediately, students may suggest finding competing sources of funding for current needs, which would allow for the continued fund raising through the candy machines while searching for viable alternatives. Such an idea allows for lateral thinking, whereby alternatives to the previously discussed suggestions are developed for consideration. This strategy helps students see that the original ideas or solutions to a problem may not always be the best option and that thinking about the alternatives to these ideas may be as productive or more so than the initial thoughts presented.

The blue hat asks participants to consider the possibilities and ideas offered and reach a consensus about how to move forward, whether through summary, conclusion, or revisiting one of the hats for further exploration (de Bono, 1999). The blue hat may be worn by the facilitator and may be used to guide which hat is used when or which hat will not be used in the discussion at hand. The blue hat represents the metacognitive thinking; the facilitator may wear the blue hat and point out when others are wearing different hats. For example, during yellow hat thinking, a student may make a critical statement, such as "I don't think that idea will work because . . .," to which the facilitator would respond, "That is black hat thinking. Let's put on our yellow hat for now, and we can revisit the black hat after we have exhausted the positives of our ideas." Or, the facilitator may use the blue hat to guide the thinking hat changes: "Let's now focus on . . ." While the teacher may model this type of thinking early in the use of the six hats method, once students understand the functions of the hats and can effectively discuss issues using them, a student may be appointed facilitator, which would allow him or her the opportunity for metacognitive functioning and growth.

Gifted students may have a plethora of ideas about a given issue or topic, and they may find it challenging to articulate these views or come to a logical decision about how to deal with such complexities of thought. Using the six thinking hats method, students are given the opportunity to simplify their thinking process and explore various facets of their thinking to make more deliberate, well-informed, logical decisions. Such opportunities can assist students in understanding the purposes of different ideas, understanding the value of each other's ideas and their own, and learning to think through a variety of options before coming to a conclusion. This methods is a rational, well-rounded approach to teaching thinking that can be of great value to students in school and life.

A Classroom Example

One lesson that became more challenging through the use of questioning techniques involved the study of Dr. Martin Luther King, Jr.'s "I Have a Dream" speech. The unit of study involved examining persuasive and rhetorical strategies in political discourse. The Rev. Jesse Jackson had recently visited the Mississippi state capital, and students examined news clippings about his trip for rhetorical strategies and persuasive techniques in their Advanced Placement language and composition class. A few days later, they took a field trip to see and hear Jackson speak and to compare his rhetorical strategies, persuasive strategies, and effect to Dr. King's famous address.

To facilitate in-class discussions, students in small groups of three shared their homework, which consisted of summaries and responses to Dr. King's speech. The teacher sat with each of the groups separately while the remaining groups worked together and discussed their homework:

Teacher: What made Jackson get a 2 and King get an 8?

Martha: I thought he just used it more effectively.

Teacher: Used what more effectively?

Martha: The repetition; I think he [King] used it more
             effectively. The repetition in Jackson's speech just
             got to me. It seemed like he was just repeating
             things over and over. The way he did it was annoy-
             ing. It didn't support what he was saying. It was
             more critical and more demanding, whereas
             Martin Luther King Jr. was just emphasizing his
             goal. And I don't see him screaming out and stuff,
             and his tone doesn't seem as harsh, which makes
             me not take offense.

Teacher: Sarah mentions in her response to your reading that
             she sees King's audience as more than African
             Americans. How can you tell this is true from
             looking back at the text?

Martha: Well, I didn't pick up on that.

Teacher: That's okay. Sarah, will you share with us what
             indicated this to you? What did he say that also
             appealed to all Americans?

Sarah: I can't remember exact words, but I think the
             metaphors he used were helpful because they
             appealed to a wide audience.

Teacher: Which metaphors are you thinking of?

Sarah: I don't know.

Lindsey: I see what she means. He uses "Americans," "God's children," "citizens." He doesn't say "Negroes" to separate them out.

Sarah: And we noticed in Jackson's speech that he chose words that suggested division like Black and White, whereas King used words to include people and bring them together.

[Another group]

Derek: [reads question slip] Are there any Americans today who capture people's imaginations of what could be?

Britton: Such as King?

Teacher: Such as King or anyone else who has a positive image about the future.

Kim: Does he?

Teacher: Does he in his speech? Does he give a positive outlook?

Derek: I'll tell you who's not the one: Jesse Jackson. He's not positive.

Teacher: Okay, well, before we answer this question, maybe we should back up and address Kim's concern. Does King present a positive outlook?

Kim: I didn't think he did. He says all these things that happened in the past. He's just picking at old wounds. I didn't think he sounded positive about much.

Britton: But, he wants his kids playing with kids of former slave owners and sitting at the table, the table of something . . . the table of freedom.

Kim: But, he brings up all these injustices. That's not positive.

Teacher: So, Kim, you see King focusing more on the negatives than the positives?

Both: Yes.

Teacher: So, you agree, too, Derek?

Derek: Yes.

Teacher: Well, tell me more about this opinion since you are agreeing with Kim.

Derek: Well, mainly what I liked about his speech was that he does say that the Blacks should just accept life and not fight back with violence. You see, if he'd have given this speech back in, say, 1870, it would have been good. If he gave this speech in, say, 1875, then it would have been a great time since slaves had just been freed. Then their freedom would have been more important.

Britton: But, in the '60s, it was also a good time because he wanted them to be able to eat in the same restaurants as White people, so it's also timely.

Derek: Yeah, I guess so. But, he was saying how we owed them for past injustices, but he was never a slave.

Teacher: So, what do you think he was saying they were owed?

Kim: I think one time it [the speech] said, "In the Constitution 'All people are created equal,' but you know, we weren't treated that way." And then he turns around and sort of waits for someone to say, "Well, we'll take care of that." He just keeps talking about things that happened.

Britton: In the beginning, he talks about Abraham Lincoln signing the Emancipation Proclamation. And then he says, "We still have segregation." And, at that time, that was true. They were still segregated.

Teacher: So, if we compare what this group is saying, Kim says King says, "You owe us, and here's why you owe us." You don't think that supports his [King's] point?

Kim: No, I think it just angers people.

Britton: [to Kim] No, he just wants equality. He's not saying they want special treatment, like affirmative action or something. He just wants equality for all races.[1]

In the first group, after listening to three students share their reactions to the speech, the teacher asked one student a follow-up question, which she answered by explaining her value system and justifying her decision.

Then, the teacher turned the discussion questions to the other two students in the group and asked them to reexamine their text with evidence from the speech to support. As the

---

[1] From "Questioning Strategies in the Gifted Classroom," by E. Shaunessy, 1999, *Gifted Child Today, 23*(5), pp. 20–21. Copyright ©1999 by Prufrock Press. Reprinted with permission.)

teacher continued the line of questioning by moving from one group to another, she gave to other groups a slip of paper containing prewritten pointed questions for them to discuss. The teacher frequently listened and questioned one group while simultaneously observing the pace and direction of other groups, distributing question slips as needed.

After working with this group, the teacher moved to the next group, where three students were answering a question given to them on a question slip. The teacher listened to their discussion and meaning making for a few minutes before posing a question that followed the direction of their conversation. Each of the students in the group expressed his or her opinions and then continued to explore the message of the speech. When the teacher sensed from students a particularly divisive stance on the issue of the message, she asked the students to restate their intent with evidence from the text.

Asking students to show evidence for their opinions by referring to the text is a method used by the Great Books Foundation. Whether reading fiction or nonfiction, these questioning techniques are useful in helping students make meaning from what they have read and, in this case, in comparing two political addresses from prominent African Americans. By posing a variety of questions, the teacher is essentially modeling the inquiry process for students, which is designed to help them imitate this process for future independent inquiries. Teachers must analyze the purposes for, types of, and reactions to questions posed.

The ultimate goal in this process is to encourage students to ask meaningful, higher level thinking questions of their peers and themselves within and beyond the classroom. While a teacher's personal reading of the texts often differs from the students' interpretations, the point of the activity is for them to examine their thinking patterns and stretch their critical thinking skills. A great deal of listening is required for the facilitator. Formulating good questions is a challenge, and the questioning process often involves the students questioning the assumptions inherent in the teacher's question.

Conclusion

Question strategies can be used from elementary through the college levels to stimulate higher level thinking skills, which are critical to the cognitive development of gifted students. Many questioning models are available for adaptation to a particular lesson, ability level, or subject area. Through the modeling of questioning and appropriate behaviors, educators and parents can encourage students to move into the role of facilitator, which is essential to the development of lifelong thinking skills and growth as independent learners who ask questions about texts, research, and life.

Web Sites About Questioning Techniques

Critical Thinking Consortium
http://www.criticalthinking.org/default.html

This site provides links to the Critical Thinking Institute, with information about the National Council for Excellence in Teaching and its standards for critical thinking, as well as products and workshops to assist educators in developing critical thinking skills in the classroom.

Socratic Teaching
http://www.cutsinger.net/socratic.html

This Web page, authored by James S. Cutsinger, a professor in the Department of Religious Studies at the University of South Carolina, contains a list of steps for implementing a Socratic seminar. Although it is designed for use in university course, it is a suitable guide for elementary and secondary educators, as well.

ENC Online: Inquiry & Problem Solving
http://www.enc.org/topics/inquiry

This site provides information about inquiry and problem solving for teachers of math and science, with links to guidance for teachers, classroom activities, and resources.

The Exploratorium: Institute for Inquiry
http://www.exploratorium.edu/IFI/index.html

This site contains articles and links to information about paradigms of using inquiry in teaching math and science.

**The Socratic Method: Teaching
by Asking Instead of Telling**
http://www.garlikov.com/Soc_Meth.html

This article by Rick Garlikov discusses how to incorporate the Socratic method; it also includes a transcript of a lesson utilizing this method.

Goodcharacter.com
http://www.goodcharacter.com/Socratic_method.html

This site provides a lesson plan for incorporating the Socratic method for the purposes of ethical and moral growth in students.

Northwest Regional Educational Laboratory: Science Inquiry Model
http://www.nwrel.org/msec/science_inq

This site describes the Science Inquiry Model and provides components of the model, teaching strategies, and resources.

Publications

Ball, W., & Brewer, P. (2000). *Socratic seminars in the block.* Larchmont, NY: Eye on Education.

Bills, L., Latham, P., & Williams, H. (2002). Encouraging all learners to think. *Mathematics Teaching, 181,* 14–16.

Black, S. (2001). Ask me a question. *American School Board Journal, 188*(5), 43–45.

Deal, D., & Sterling, D. (1997). Kids ask the best questions. *Educational Leadership, 54,* 61–63.

Elder, L., & Paul, R. (1998). The role of Socratic questioning in thinking, learning, teaching. *The Clearing House 71*(5), 297–301.

Feldman, S. (2003). The right line of questioning. *Teaching PreK–8, 33*(4), 8.

Galas, C. (1999). The never–ending story? Questioning strategies for the information age. *Learning and Leading With Technology, 26*(7), 10–13.

Guilford, J. P. (1967). *The nature of human intelligence.* New York: McGraw-Hill.

Hannel, G., & Hannel, L. (1998). The seven steps to critical thinking: A practical application of critical thinking skills. *NASSP Bulletin, 82*(598), 87–93.

Harris, R. (2000). Questioning techniques in student-centered classrooms. *The Clearing House, 74*(1), 25–26.

Polite, V., & Adams, A. (1997). Critical thinking and values clarification through Socratic seminars. *Urban Education, 32,* 256–278.

Shoeman, S. (1997). Using the Socratic method in secondary teaching. *NASSP Bulletin, 81*(587), 19–21.

Additional Resources

For more information about Junior Great Books, call (800) 222-5870 or visit http://www.greatbooks.org.

References

Ball, W., & Brewer, P. (2000). *Socratic seminars in the block.* Larchmont, NY: Eye on Education.

Bloom, B. S. (Ed.). (1956). *Taxonomy of educational objectives: The classification of educational goals. Handbook I: Cognitive domain.* New York: Longmans, Green.

Callahan, C. (1978). *Developing creativity in the gifted and talented.* Reston, VA: Council for Exceptional Children.

Daniels, S. (1997). Creativity in the classroom: Characteristics, climate, and curriculum. In N. Colangelo & G. A. Davis (Eds.), *Handbook of gifted education* (2nd ed., pp. 300–301). Boston: Allyn and Bacon.

de Bono, E. (1970). *Lateral thinking: Creativity step by step.* New York: Harper and Row.

de Bono, E. (1999). *Six thinking hats.* Boston: Back Bay.

Feldhusen, J. (1994). Thinking skills and curriculum development. In J. VanTassel-Baska (Ed.), *Comprehensive curriculum for gifted learners* (pp. 301–324). Boston: Allyn and Bacon.

Gallagher, J. J. (1985). *Teaching the gifted child*. Boston: Allyn and Bacon.

Gallagher, J. J., & Gallagher, S. A. (1994). *Teaching the gifted child*. Boston: Allyn and Bacon.

Glenn, R. (1997). Scamper for student creativity. *Education Digest, 62*(6), 67–68.

Grambo, G. (1997). Questions in your classroom. *Gifted Child Today, 20*(3), 42–43.

Guilford, J. P. (1967). *The nature of human intelligence*. New York: McGraw-Hill.

Hunkins, F. P. (1976). *Involving students in questioning*. Boston: Allyn and Bacon.

Hyman, R. (1979). *Strategic questioning*. Englewood Cliffs, NJ: Prentice Hall.

Krathwohl, D., Bloom, B., & Masia, B. (1964). *Taxonomy of educational objectives. Handbook II: The affective domain*. New York: McKay.

Letzter, F. (1982). Meeting the special needs of the gifted and creative student in the world history classroom. *Social Education, 46*, 195–199.

Maker, C. J., & Nielson, A. (1996). *Curriculum development and teaching strategies for gifted learners*. Austin, TX: PRO-ED.

Manktelow, J. (2003). *Mind tools: Essential skills for an excellent career*. West Sussex, England: Mind Tools.

Parker, J. (1989). *Instructional strategies for teaching the gifted*. Boston: Allyn and Bacon.

Patterson, J. (1973). *Why doesn't an igloo melt inside? A handbook for teachers of the academically gifted and talented*. Memphis, TN: Memphis City School System. (ERIC Document Reproduction Service No. ED083 760)

Pollack, H. (1988). *Questioning strategies to encourage critical thinking*. (ERIC Document Reproduction Service No. ED297 210)

Schwartz, B., & Millar, G. (1996). *You are what you ask: The power of teaching students questioning skills for enabling thinking*. Paper presented at the annual Sage conference, Calgary,

Alberta, Canada. (ERIC Document Reproduction Service No. ED408 744)

Shaunessy, E. (1999). Questioning techniques in the gifted classroom. *Gifted Child Today, 23*(5), 14–21.

Strasser, B. (1967). The use of questions as an aspect of a teacher's behavior. In J. Gowan, G. Demos, & E. Torrence (Eds.), *Creativity: Its educational implications* (pp. 207–209). New York: Wiley.

Will, H. (1987). Asking good follow-up questions. *Gifted Child Today, 10*(4), 32–34.

Winocur, S., & Maurer, P. (1997). Critical thinking and gifted students: Using IMPACT to improve teaching and learning. In N. Colangelo & G. A. Davis (Eds.), *Handbook of gifted education* (2nd ed., pp. 308–317). Boston: Allyn and Bacon.

Wolf, D. (1987, Winter). The art of questioning. *Academic Connections,* 1–7. Retrieved May 25, 2004, from http://www.exploratorium.com/IFI/resources/workshops/artofquestioning.html

About the Author

Elizabeth Shaunessy is assistant professor of gifted education and the coordinator of the graduate program in gifted education in the Department of Special Education at the University of South Florida in Tampa. She graduated in 2003 from The University of Southern Mississippi, where she worked on two federal grants to assist educators and policymakers in screening and identifying culturally diverse gifted children and gifted/disabled students. Her interests in gifted education include teaching strategies, instructional technology, gifted/disabled students, culturally diverse students, policy, and secondary options for the gifted. She has provided staff development to school districts; some of the topics addressed in these professional development opportunities included critical thinking skills, programming options for gifted secondary students, identifying and serving culturally diverse gifted students, challenging students in the block schedule, and reading strategies for all learners. She taught language arts in the secondary classroom for 9 years.